AUTHOR'S

Before I begin I am assuming that all of my readers have access to a computer with a broadband internet connection. You need to be in a position to not only watch races live, but also have a stable and fast enough internet connection to back horses in running. You also need to watch historical videos of races, as I believe, although studying the form book plays a major part in the life of all successful gamblers, it is preferable to watch a video of any race which can then regularly form part of your day to day studying.

Many internet bookmakers today, once you have opened an account, will give you access to watch live any race on which you have placed a bet with them, and many offer a video library of past races, again fully accessible to account holders. *At the Races* also provides videos of past races to anyone registered with the site, but only from the race courses that they broadcast from.

In the following pages what you will not get are tips for particular races or a system that enables you to make selections from a daily newspaper's racing section. What I will provide is a roadmap that if followed religiously, will I believe enable you to operate in a more professional manner, and to win money from your betting year after year. Before I begin I will tell you that if you follow my advice, I do strongly believe that your betting will be profitable, but and this is a big **BUT**, you must be prepared to put in the work to achieve results. I believe it was Sam Goldwyn who said *"It's funny but the harder I work, the luckier I get"*, nonetheless this is the mantra you must adopt if you are serious about gambling for profit and not for fun. However if you are not prepared to put in the effort, I suggest you don't waste your time reading any further.

SECTION 1   INTRODUCTION

SECTION 2   10 GOLDEN RULES

SECTION 3   SPECIALISE, SPECIALISE, SPECIALISE

SECTION 4   BET NOT ONLY TO WIN, BUT TO AVOID LOSING

SECTION 5   THERE IS NO SUCH THING AS A FUN BET

SECTION 6   BUILD A BETTING BANK

SECTION 7   TREAT YOUR BETTING AS A BUSINESS

SECTION 8   NEVER BET WHAT YOU CAN'T AFFORD TO LOSE

SECTION 9   LET DISCIPLINE BE YOUR WATCHWORD

SECTION 10   DO NOT FOLLOW OTHER'S TIPS BLINDLY, ACCEPT RESPONSIBILITY

SECTION 11   EQUIPE YOURSELF WITH THE TOOLS TO SUCCEED

SECTION 12   YOUR OWN PERSONAL DATABASE

SECTION 13   DO A THROUGH JOB – STUDYING FORM

SECTION 14   MAKE USE OF BOOKMAKERS SPECIAL DEALS

SECTION 15   WHAT IS VALUE

SECTION 16   FOUR IN A ROW – A NEW METHOD

SECTION 17   HOW I STUDY FORM

SECTION 18   WHAT TYPE OF GAMBLER YOU NEED TO BE

INTRODUCTION

I have been backing horses since the age of fourteen, over 50 years. My grandfather sparked my interest as I spent most Saturday afternoons with him, watching *Grandstand* on the television, whilst my parents went shopping. My grandfather liked the occasional bet on the horses and had backed them long before betting shops became legal. During the 1940s and early '50s, his son, and my uncle, Eddie, had worked as a bookie's runner. Over the course of a century, the bookies' runner, who took bets on street corners and at the factory gates on behalf of the local gamblers, became a familiar figure. There was even specialist technology to ensure the security of this multi-million-pound illegal industry, in the form of the clock bag, which locked securely and recorded the time when it was shut. Betting 'after time' was thus almost impossible.

The enemy of the runners was the local beat policeman. The runners always had a lookout who would warn of the approaching cop. The runners would then disappear until the PC had plodded by.

Bookies' runners flourished and optimistic people like my grandfather with, perhaps, just a shilling (5 pence) or two to spend would speculate some of it on a horserace, just as many today regularly spend pounds on Lottery tickets or in betting shops and, of course, on the latest phenomenon online gambling, in all its various guises. However, going back to that time, everything changed for the betting man, when in May 1961 licensed betting offices arrived on the high streets.

One Saturday I asked my grandfather if I could have a bet. He said 'How much can you afford to lose?' to which I replied, 'Two bob' (10 pence).

'OK. Pick out three horses,' he said, passing me the racing page of the newspaper.

I duly selected three horses and he wrote out a bet for me, which were three 6d (2.5 pence) doubles and one 6d treble. He advised me if I was to see any of my money returned I would have to have at least two of the three horses win. After he returned from the bookies, we sat down to watch *Grandstand*. Two of the three races I had selected were being televised and I was able to cheer wildly as both of my horses won, and my grandfather informed me that I had won 12 shillings already, with the third horse still to run. The final part of *Grandstand* was the football and racing results round-up, and much to my grandfather's disbelief my third horse also won, and for my two-bob bet I had a return of £6 2/-. That was the day I became hooked on horse racing and gambling, a passion that has remained with me throughout my life.

It's fair to say that overall, since I started gambling, and before the start of the new Century I probably have had more losing years than winning ones, although I did enjoy some good wins, during the successful years. However, I have posted a profit every year since the year 1997 due mainly to my refined systematic approach, aided by the introduction of betting exchanges (more of that later).

The history of my betting accounts from the year 1997, are detailed in section four.

THE 10 GOLDEN RULES

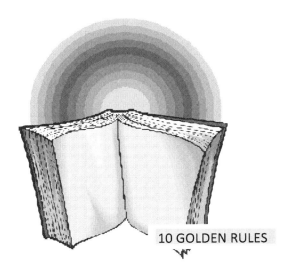

10 GOLDEN RULES

- BET NOT TO WIN, BUT TO AVOID LOSING
- FORGET HAVING BETS FOR FUN
- BUILD A BETTING BANK
- TREAT YOUR BETTING AS A BUSINESS
- NEVER BET WHAT YOU CAN'T AFFORD TO LOSE
- LET DISCIPLINE BE YOUR WATCHWORD
- DO NOT FOLLOW OTHER'S TIPS BLINDLY - ACCEPT RESPONSIBILITY
- EQUIPE YOURSELF WITH THE TOOLS TO SUCCEED
- BUILD YOUR OWN DATABASE OF HORSES
- SPECIALISE SPECIALISE SPECIALISE

SPECIALISE – SPECIALISE - SPECIALISE

I want to go into detail about the golden rules, and I will start with the last rule "specialise, specialise, specialise".

How many people do you know that are champions or Olympic medal winners in more than one discipline? I know the answer and it is hardly any. I believe therefore that if you are to win regularly at gambling, then you **MUST** specialise.

Around twenty years ago I analysed my bets, and found that overall I was winning on bets on National Hunt Racing and losing on Flat Racing, so from that day on I stopped backing horses on the flat.

It wasn't long after this that I analysed my bets further and found my bets on horses jumping hurdles, in the main were producing losing bets, so I then restricted my bets to chasers only.

Since the year 2000 my speciality has been refined even further, and in my case I only back in chases where the highest rated horse has a rating of 115 or **less**. The only exception to this is long distance chases in excess of 3ml 1 furlong, as my records show I am good at finding winners in staying events, regardless of the class of the horses involved. I also back in Hunter Chasers, regardless of their official rating. It is fair to say that very view tend to involve horses above a 115 rating, as horses rated above 115 are in the main ex handicapers who are in the twilight of their careers. You may have guessed from the name "Pointerman", that this is an area where I have extensive knowledge. I will detail where my knowledge of Point to Pointers, has proved very beneficial later.

I must stress this again. It's important that you realise that I have not had a losing year since I developed this strategy.

Now I am not for one moment, suggesting you follow my speciality area, but what I am suggesting is that you develop your own speciality area, after analysing your bets for at least six months.

This may seem like a lot of work, but if you take the time to carry out a thorough analysis of your bets, by recording all relevant data for six months to highlight your strengths and weaknesses, it will I believe provide major benefits for your future betting.

The benefits I derive from my speciality area is that I am aware of most of the horses contesting the races I gamble on, and in these races jumping ability is more of an asset, than in races in grade one courses, for example. This is mainly because many lowly rated horses are very poor jumpers, and a good jumper racing in this class, can win against higher rated horses based solely on his ability to jump a fence.

This means of course apart from the long distance races I seldom have runners in my speciality area at the Grade One courses.

The Cheltenham Festival is one of the largest betting meetings of the year when millions change hands. To find winners here is difficult, most of the horses have considerable ability, many are proficient jumpers and all races are hotly contested, often with many runners. Small fields tend to be rare and where there is a small field it generally headed by a very short priced favourite, and finding a value bet is unlikely.

If I can take you back to the festival of March 2011, on the first day there was a meeting at *Sedgefield*, and I was involved in a race, as it was within my speciality area, that race being a 0-85 handicap over 2m 4f, with 11 runners, which was won by *Humbel Times* at 9-1 (my selection). The following day at the festival there was a 2m 110y hurdle grade 3, with no less than 23 runners, won by *What a Charm* at 9-1.

Now which winner was the more difficult to find? I think the answer is obvious. **Remember – Remember – Remember**, a 9-1 winner at a lowly track returns exactly the same profit as a 9-1 winner at a Grade one course.

Now it might be of course that after analysing your bets, you reach the conclusion that most of your profit comes from your bets on Grade one courses, so that may become your area of expertise, but I seriously doubt it, as races at this level are very competitive.

The other great advantage of specialising is you can spend more time studying the races which fall in your area of expertise. When I looked at all races and all meetings many years ago, I would try desperately to study the form in every single race. Just how much time can you spend on worthwhile form study if you are trying to accommodate a typical of 3 to 4 meetings a day with six races on average at each meeting? On a normal day, I will study between one to three races a session, with a fair number of blank days between, when there are no races I have an interest in. I have been known to spend as much as four hours studying one race including reviewing videos of each runner, and you won't be surprised to learn that the longer I spend on a race, the luckier I get.

I can't stress enough the benefits of specialisation, so I will give you a further example to think about. If you ever watch the television show *Mastermind*, you will frequently see a contestant who when questioned on their specialised subject, will not get one question wrong. Following this when they go to the general knowledge round they score very poorly. It is much easier when you are concentrating on a narrow field of information to become an expert than if you try to be all encompassing, knowing everything about everything. Do not make the mistake of becoming *a Jack of all trades, Master of none.*

I do believe that if you follow a simple set of rules that whether you are specialising in horse racing, greyhound racing or football, the same golden rules may apply.

However my success is achieved by only backing on NH horse racing, and nothing else, so all of what follows of course relates to NH horse racing.

BET NOT TO WIN, BUT TO AVOID LOSING.

I can hear one or two of you asking what on earth is he talking about.

With the introduction of the betting exchanges in early 2000, it became possible to lay bets to lose as well as to win. Over 60% of all my bets are what are known as "matched bets".

For example if I back a horse at 20-1, and am able to lay him after my winning bet has been accepted at odds of 10-1, then if he wins I have backed a 10-1 winner, but if he loses I have protected my stake.

Around 4 years ago I had a run of bad luck that most reading this will have also probably experienced at some time. I had a run of no less than 17 consecutive horses that finished second, all backed to win. Now before the introduction of the betting exchanges, two things would have happened, I would have lost a considerable amount of money, and my confidence would have been shot to pieces. However fifteen of these were matched bets, so the losses were small, and my confidence wasn't so badly affected.

I should mention at this point that most of my matched bets, take place during the running of the race. You should be aware that you can place both a bet and a lay, whilst the race is happening. There is however around A few seconds delay between the pictures arriving on your screen, from the racecourse, so you need to treat all bets with caution.

I firmly believe one of the keys to a successful betting strategy is the ability to lay off ones bets.

What follows is a record of my bets since the year 2007, comparing winning months against losing months, and the overall outcome of profit/ loss, for each year. I have then calculated the average for the years 2007 to 2016 inclusive.

Year	Winning Months	Losing Months	Points/Profit - Loss
2007	9	3	321
2008	6	6	802
2009	8	4	162
2010	5	7	79
2011	9	3	45
2012	6	6	148
2013	8	4	302
2014	10	2	402
2015	4	8	355
2016	7	5	903
TOTALS	72	48	3117
AVERAGE	7.2	4.8	311.7

As you can see from the table overall my winning months are much greater, when compared with my losing months. On analysing the results in more detail, if I were to assume all my matched bets were either straight winning or losing bets, although I would benefit from the extra returns on my winning bets the effect of my losing bets, would produce a ratio of 50-50 when winning and losing months are compared. Much more important however is that I would have suffered three losing years during the period analysed.

I believe this clearly demonstrates the strength of my strategy of protecting stakes whenever possible.

You will also notice that my profit for some years, is not as good as other years, and part of the reason for this is caused by the fact that I have had bookmaker's accounts closed or restricted, particularly with regard to those bookmakers who offer early bird prices on the following day's racing.

I have found a number of ways around that problem in the last two years, but my methods are not something I can't disclose.

A question that is regularly put to racing pundits, is should you back odds on favourites. My position is that I will never back odds on favourites, but I have been known to lay them. Your success rate needs to be off the scale if you regularly back odds on, and I wouldn't advise it. If you operate the way I do by matching my bets wherever possible, the shorter the price the harder it becomes to lay the bet and still make a reasonable profit. Very few of my bets are under 3-1, as it is rare that horses at these odds provide value, although I have occasionally backed horses at 6-4 when on my tissue, I believe they should be 1-3.

THERE IS NO SUCH THING AS A FUN BET

Many years ago I was a member of Towcester Race Club, and would attend all of their meetings, and I was a regular racegoer to many other courses within a 100 mile radius of my home. Initially I would study long and hard the preceding evening, and on the day would have a bet in every single race, many which I would classify as fun bets, where my instinct was they would probably lose, but it would add to the excitement of the day, and they just might win.

If you are serious about making money from gambling, forget all about fun bets, they will decrease any profit from your bets proper, and again can have an effect on levels of confidence.

When I visit a racecourse today, I not only will have a strategy of which races to get involved with, but what odds I require from the horse I wish to back. Should I be unable to get the odds I require, **I WILL NOT HAVE A BET**. I can happily watch every race without having a bet, but I never consider it to be a wasted day, because I am able to evaluate the race/s in which I intended to bet, and perhaps will find a horse who I may add to my personal database (more of that later).

BUILD A BETTING BANK

If you're serious about making money from gambling, you must separate your day to day money from your gambling funds. How big the bank needs to be depends on what you can afford, and what amounts you usually bet.

When I started my betting bank around 20 years ago, I started with a lump sum, in my case it was only £500, and as I was working at the time I would add a further £80 per month, from my day to day monies, which was more than affordable for me at that time. As soon as my bank had reached £2,000 I decided that was sufficient and did not add any further monies from my earnings.

Now if you haven't got available funds to start a betting bank, I suggest you stop gambling immediately and use the monies you would have gambled to build a betting bank. One way of assuring you don't deplete your bank too quickly is I would advise that perhaps you calculate your bets as a percentage of your betting bank, at 5 or 10 %.

Each year my target was to double my betting bank, and any surplus was withdrawn and used to enhance my standard of living (cars, holidays, hi-fi equipment etc.) My own betting bank now runs to five figures (after allowing for regular withdrawals, and I now have no need to add further sums to the bank from my regular profits, as the size of the bank will ensure I could easily survive the odd losing year. However I very much doubt I will ever experience a losing year, so confident am I about my own abilities, and the power of my betting strategy.

I would also advise that you do not leave large cash sums with bookmakers; it is very easy if you always carry balances with bookmakers to leave it until you need it, by leaving your winnings in your account. It is probably not much of a risk to leave monies with all of the big high street bookies, though I would suggest you draw of any surplus over £500, with the exception of the exchanges, as for them by virtue of needing large enough funds to cover any lays you may offer, you will require a much higher sum in your account.

I offer this advice as during my betting life I have no less than three bookmakers go under, all owing me money which I was unable to recover.

About a year ago I allocated a small sum to a second betting bank for a new strategy, and I will detail how this operates in a separate section.

TREAT YOUR BETTING AS A BUSINESS

The golden rule here is to document every single bet, as you need to be aware where your profits are coming from and where you are losing. I firstly have a day book and in that I write the details of any horse I have backed, together with details of any lay, and the origin of the bet, i.e. whether the bet was placed on the betting exchanges or with a bookmaker and if so which one.

In the evening, after racing for the day has ended, I enter the financial details into a spread sheet, across the top are the months of the year, and down the left hand side the days of the month. Therefore each day has a cell in which is entered the profit or loss from that day. Along the bottom of the sheet are the totals for each individual month with a running total of the profit or loss.

I also measure the proceeding year's monthly totals against the current year's monthly totals which show my performance year on year. Each individual bet has a bets breakdown sheet, in which I enter all relevant information, but you do what you feel comfortable with, providing you are fully aware of your winning or losing position every single day.

All expenses incurred in my business need to be set against profits, so each month I would advise that you deduct the cost of racing literature and membership expenses. I do this with everything, with the exception of my subscription to the *Racing Channel*, because if I never had another bet, I would still want to watch National Hunt racing, as to me it is a pleasure.

It is vital as with every business that you control expenses, so do you need to buy the *Racing Post* every day?, or would it be more economical to take a *Racing Post* basic membership and do your studying via the internet.

In my opinion the full membership of the *Racing Post* via the internet is a waste of money, as all it adds is a video archive, which you can get for free elsewhere, and access to various tipsters, which if you have confidence in your abilities, you will not need.

I will give full details of what I believe I need later, and this may provide some idea as to what you may need.

LET DISCIPLINE BE YOUR WATCHWORD

I honestly believe that to be successful in any walk of life you need to exact discipline over yourself to ensure success. This means that you will never again place a "fun bet", **not even once**.

You will religiously document all bets and their outcome, keeping your accounts up to date on a daily basis. Should you experience a losing day, you will not tell yourself that it would be OK not to document the bet as it was only minor. You document **EVERYTHING**.

I would advise you to read the Golden Rules daily and if you need to motivate yourself surround the area where you do your horse form studying with motivational statements.

I have photocopies of winning bets and statements on a pin board above the desk where I normally study, just to remind myself of past successes.

Another great motivator for me is that all around my house are oil paintings of racehorses, which I commissioned after they had provided me with winning days not to be forgotten. For example I have oils of both Red Maurader and Little Suspect, both

Grand National winners, who supplied me with two of my best and most profitable days in racing.

I also have the following poem, which I wrote after a particular bad day, where no less than four hours of studying the form resulted in a losing day.

> *Walk away,*
> *It's just another day*
> *Win or lose*
> *Up or down*
> *The bet's been struck*
> *The wager laid*
> *Money lost – money made*
> *I can't always win I'll sometimes lose*
> *But whatever I do, whatever I say*
> *I must remember – to walk away*
> *It's just another day.*

If I was asked to describe what is needed to be a successful gambler in one word, that word would be "discipline".

NEVER BET WHAT YOU CAN'T AFFORD TO LOSE

This may sound simplistic, but there is no such thing as a certainty in any form of gambling. Almost every week on betfair some punter will lay 1,000-1,for a horse trailing the field and some lucky punter will take the bet. There is then a series of events that occur (horses falling, or refusing, taking the wrong course etc. etc.) and the horse ends up winning. Why on earth anyone would lay odds of 1,000-1 to win a few pounds. They only have to be wrong more than once in 1,000 bets to lose big time. Providing you have a betting bank separate from the main source of income, then you should never spend the mortgage or rent money down the bookies.

Should you be unlucky enough to lose the vast majority of your betting bank, then you should cease betting immediately, and deposit what you can afford to your betting bank, until you have sufficient to carry on.

This is very much where your new found discipline comes to the fore. Under no circumstances borrow monies from other areas of your budget. If you have allocated a monthly or weekly sum to go to your betting bank from your disposable income, that's fine, but you should never risk problems in other parts of your life to fund your betting.

DO NOT FOLLOW OTHER'S TIPS BLINDLY, ACCEPT RESPONSIBILITY

Personally I will not take account of anyone's tips, although I am aware that journalists like *"Pricewise"* in the *"Racing Post"*, do have quite a formidable track record. I am not very happy when on the rare occasion one of his tips is in a long distance chase, and he is advising a horse I intend to bet. I only place a bet when I believe the price on offer to be value, and often the fact that he has tipped the horse, sends the odds crashing. If you choose to follow a racing tipster, that is your decision, so if the horse loses, it is not the tipster's fault, but yours, because you chose to follow them.

Similarly when placing a bet that you have selected it is unlikely to be the Jockey or Trainers fault if it loses, though on the rare occasion this may be the case. No indeed 90% of the time it is your fault, because you did not do enough groundwork, or you overlooked some critical piece of information.

Remember also horses are no different from the others living on this planet, in that we can all feel ill or have an off day. Never write a horse off because of one bit of poor form. Replay the video of the race and see if there was any obvious reason for the unexplained poor display. If nothing is obvious, it could be just an off day – it happens.

EQUIPE YOURSELF WITH THE TOOLS TO SUCCEED

Here are listed, the books and information that I feel I need to ensure that my business is a success. Yours of course could be different, depending on your area of speciality. For the purposes of this exercise I am assuming your area of speciality is similar to mine.

- A basic membership to the *Racing Post* on the internet
- *Timeform's – Chasers & Hurdlers Annual*
- Membership of *At The Races* web site (free). This allows you to look at video recordings of races broadcast on *At The Races;* also their race cards give *Timeform* comments on all of the runners.
- An internet account with ALL of the leading bookmakers.
- An internet account with a betting exchange (*Betfair* is the largest)
- Membership of *Viewpoint* (this gives videos and form guides for point to point races in England, Scotland and Wales.
- A package with a satellite or cable supplier which as part of the package supplies coverage of *At The Races* channel

- An account with the *Racing Channel,* so together with *At The Races*, you are able to watch all racing live.
- *The Point to Point & Hunter Chase Form and Statistics* (available direct from *Weatherbys*, each season.
- There are also further publications which will give you information and trainer's comments on their horses, such as John Morris's *"Jumping Prospects"*, Marten Julian's *"Dark Horses", Timeform's "Horse to follow"* and others that I have no experience of.

To put more meat on the bones, the *Racing Post* comes out daily and I believe is an excellent source of form and information regarding any days racing. If however you find the cost prohibitive, (over £2 per day at the time of writing) you could take a basic membership with the Racing Post website, which will supply most of the information available in the paper, but via your computer screen, and at a much lower annual cost. Another option is the *Racing Post Weekender,* which gives details of all meetings between Wednesday and Sunday of each week's racing.

Opening accounts with all the major bookmakers is vital as many price up some races the evening before racing, and some very healthy early prices are available. Beware though no bookmakers like regular winners and as I have already documented I have had more than one major bookmaker close my account. One of them was one of the biggest bookies trading, and suffice to say "he was no friend of mine". Of those bookmakers that have not closed my account, most now restrict my bets, and I have no doubt this will shock most people reading this, but these events actually happened. I wanted to back a horse which was on offer with two large bookmakers at 25-1 (I believed it should have been around a 12-1 shot), the evening before the race, and all I was looking for was a £30 win bet. Having signed in to my account and attempted to place the bet with the first bookmaker, I was refused the full bet and offered a stake of £2.50p. The second was much more generous and actually offered me a maximum stake of £4. Now both of these gutless bookmakers both advertise regularly on television, offering all sorts of enticements to open an account with them. The do however forget to inform you that you are only welcome providing you are going to do your utmost to lose regularly. The worst of the lot is Ladbrokes who have limited my stake to £1, yes this is not a misprint £1. I can't stress this enough, today's bookmakers are only interested in regular losers. If you regularly win money from them even if is only the hundreds, they will restrict your bets or close your account. They are spineless as well as gutless.

You therefore need if possible to stay under their radar, so if you want to place a £100 bet, ten £10 bets spread over 10 bookmakers is less of a risk then one bet of £100, always providing you can find ten bookmakers to accept your bets. These may sound like small sums, to some of you, but believe me any bet at £50 or above is passed to a trading manager, and if you have winning form, they may pass all of your bets for acceptance by a trading manager. Furthermore if you are a regular winner, they will close your account entirely, or restrict your stakes, to such an extent that it's hardly worth having the bet.

Yes they all talk of millions of pounds, but in reality all regular winning punters frighten them, regardless of the size of the bet.

Of course no such restrictions apply to the *Betting Exchanges*, but on many occasions some of the bookmaker's early evening prices are never available on the betting exchanges. The only restriction of the exchanges is that you must have sufficient monies deposited in your account to cover any bet or lay you wish to place. Unfortunately for most successful gamblers this is the only place they can get a bet, once the gutless one's have closed their accounts.

Back to the selection of your bets, if also you are like me and occasionally want a break from the computer screen, you can get your race form in hard copy in two ways.

Raceform Ltd, produce a publication which you can subscribe to called *"The Jumps Form Book"*, there is also an equivalent publication for Flat racing, or the *Weekender,* has a form pull-out, for both codes of racing, which can be used to build your own hard copy form book.

If you find that purchasing all of the books and memberships is more than you can afford initially, then build up your tools gradually, but first and foremost you must be in a position to study form be it either by way of the *Racing Post Weekender's* pull-outs, or the Racing Post by hard copy or via the internet. If your friends or relatives have no idea of what to buy you for Xmas, give them a list of the racing books you would like.

In my opinion one of the best publications for giving useful information is *Timeform's Chasers & Hurdlers Annual,* which gives details of every horse which ran in the previous National Hunt season. If you can afford to add this to your winner finding armoury, it is worth every penny of the £75 it costs at the time of writing.

Many young horses today graduate through the point to point field, so I believe that if your area of speciality is jump racing, then you must have access to the point to point form. This is readily available with the annual from *Weatherbys*, but if like me you prefer to watch the horses in action, you can do this by taking out a membership with *Viewpoint,* and many of the point to point races are available to watch in their historical video database (the quality is not good, as in the main the videos are shot by amateurs), together with the form for horses contesting point to points.

What always I find hard to explain, is why none of the bookmakers in my opinion, have a specialist in English and Irish point to point racing. There are many examples of Grand National winners and Gold Cup winners who started their racing in point to point racing.

Time and Time again I see horses racing under National Hunt Rules, who have very sound point to point or Hunter Chase form, but are five to ten points or sometimes more, overpriced with the bookmakers.

One of the best examples of this is the 1998 Gold Cup winner Cool Dawn, who was bought by the amateur rider Dido Harding for £7,000. She rode him and won on him in Ladies point to point races, but to be brutally honest the horse would have ran just as well if he had a bag of concrete strapped to the saddle as Dido was no Tony McCoy. He had finished 2nd in the Foxhunters at Cheltenham, the Amateur's Gold Cup. Miss Harding then stepped down from riding him and he ran third in the Irish Grand National piloted by Conor O'Dwyer. Miss Harding rode him one last time at the start of an enforced lay off due to injury, at the beginning of a new season.

Prior to the Gold Cup he won his third race at Ascot under 12 stone, and flopped in his next race with a shoulder injury being given as the explanation.

He was available at odds of 40-1 and 33-1 before the big day, odds I was more than happy to accept. His starting price was 25-1, in my mind still overpriced, and Andrew Thornton gave him a fine ride to lead almost all the way.

The biggest ever rank outsider to win the Gold Cup was Norton's Coin in 1990. If it wasn't enough that Norton's Coin started the race as a 100/1 afterthought, he did so by beating a field that included the legendary Desert Orchid, who was the odds-on favourite.

Norton's Coin was only entered in the Gold Cup because his owner had missed the deadline for a lesser value handicap race at the Cheltenham festival. Sirrell Griffiths, who also trained the horse, only set off for Cheltenham on the morning of the race, after milking the cows on his farm in West Wales. Little did he know that his horse would hold off a challenge from Dessie and Toby Tobias to clinch an unlikely victory.

Here again is a horse with sound point to point form and even his Rules form prior to running in the Gold Cup, was sound, having finished third over the Cheltenham fences at odds of 66-1.

Now nobody would claim he was a good thing in that Gold Cup to beat Desert Orchard, but his odds of 100-1 were seriously overpriced. In my book I made him a 33-1 shot. I had only my minimum stake on him, believing he might just get placed, and the rest is history.

YOUR OWN PERSONAL DATABASE

Often when watching a race either on a racecourse or a video of a race, you will notice perhaps a horse which ran and jumped well for 2ml of a 3ml race and was eventually pulled up. It may be that your reading of the race, leads you to suspect he could win over 2ml. How many times has this happened and when the horse next ran it didn't register with you, and it wasn't until the next day when looking through the previous day's results, the penny drops and he has won a 2ml race at odds of 16-1.

To avoid such things happening you need to build your own database of horses to watch for, by entering the details on your own database, sorting it into alphabetical order, and checking each race in your specialisation area with your database to see if any are runners.

If you don't want to waste your time checking your database each day, there are free websites around, where you can enter details of the horses in question and the next occasion they run, you are sent an e-mail informing you of the details of the race they are down to run in.

For example *At the Races*, offer just such a service, for its members (it is free to join), for up to 100 horses and there are other sites on the internet who offer an unlimited number of entries. If you subscribe to a membership with the *Racing Post* website, you will have access to something called *Horse Tracker*, which enable you to enter a horse's details and when it is either entered or declared to run, you will receive an e-mail informing you of where and when the horse is planned to run. I would also advise at the end of every week's racing to examine in detail the notebook comments for the races in your specialization area, and add to your database the name of any horse that finished outside the placed horses, with a positive comment, which you agree with after having viewed the video of the race.

It takes only a short time each week to add your new entries on your database to whichever site you have chosen, to manage them for you, and it will save you hours of time in the future, with no possibility of missing a winner.

DO A THOROUGH JOB IN YOUR STUDYING OF FORM

Now if I am teaching my granny to suck eggs in this section then I apologise in advance. There is more to looking at each horse in any race, where it finished and how it ran in its last race.

I have listed all the components I believe you should consider.

- The distance of the race, previous experience.
- The ground conditions, will they act on it?
- Have any of the runners got course form?
- Record of the jockey riding it.
- Is the trainer in form? and has he/she got course form?
- If the horse is running for the first time, this season, what is their first time out record?
- Does the time since its last race fit with the horses running pattern? some horses need longer to recover from hard races.
- Pay particular attention to horses that have pulled up, where it is an unusual occurrence, look at the video of the race for an explanation. (some of my biggest priced winners have come from following through on this aspect of form)

- Is the horse wearing blinkers, cheek pieces or a tongue tie for the first time?
- Has the horse changed stables since its last run?
- Is the horse dropping in class? Time and time again you will find horses that have been running at higher class courses, and finishing outside the placed horses, and also falling in the handicap, then going on to win, at generous odds, when racing in a lower class race.
- Have you read in the racing press or on the web, that the horse has had a breathing operation, since its last race? This is just the sort of information, which should be entered into your own database.

If you make the above part of your regular studying of form, your opportunities for finding winners will improve greatly.

I would also like to expand the point about horses dropping in class, take careful note of any horse that has been running in let's say class 3 and 4 races, and his handicap mark has been steadily dropping. Then they appear for the first time in a class 5 race because their handicap rating has fallen far enough for them to contest these races. Time and time again you will find these horses have an upturn in form and win their race, many at good odds.

It is probably prudent to add, that I took early retirement in order that I could spend more time studying, and for me that decision was a good one. If however you are working, I can appreciate that it is difficult to fit in form study with everything else you need to do. This is the point that you have to show determination and discipline, by perhaps forgetting about the television, and devoting some evenings to form study. Also if you are as I suggest applying specialization to your betting, then there will be many days when no races fall within your area of specialization, and this is the time to relax and recharge your batteries.

If you are a punter who feels the need to bet every day, then you're betting is becoming a compulsion and can eventually only lead to joining the ranks of the long term losers.

On the other hand there is nothing wrong with spending your blank days by looking at recordings of past races, and observing the horses in running, when I have no doubt you will find horses to add to your personal data bank.

For me there is no greater thrill, than to have spent many hours studying a race, coming up with my selection and then watching the race unfold exactly as I believed it would with my selection winning.

Various articles have been published over the years determining what percentage of gamblers win. With regard to horse racing from the articles I have read over the years, most regular winning professionals are between 1% and 4%.

My firm belief is that if you wish to join their ranks you must be prepared to put in the work, glancing through a national newspaper and trying to accurately recall what horses have passed your radar, without studying the race in detail is the road to disaster.

MAKE USE OF BOOKMAKERS SPECIAL DEALS

Be aware of bookmaker's special deals as they can help increase your betting bank with free money, and increased benefits.

When you open either an internet account or a mobile telephone account, most bookies will add a percentage of your initial deposit, which can gain you anything from an extra £5, up to £200. So make use of this when setting up your betting accounts.

Once your accounts are up and running, watch out for periodic offers.

Bet 365 has from time to time offered to increase any deposit to an account, by 25%, up to a maximum of a £100 bonus. If therefore you deposit £400, they add an extra £100. This is **free money;** the only obligation you have is that you must play through your deposit and bonus three times before you can withdraw both. If you are a regular gambler it won't take too long to achieve this, and where else would you receive 25% interest on a deposit.

Most of the large bookmakers offer to pay whichever is the greater, between an early price you have taken, and the starting price (regrettably this benefit has been withdrawn from my bets, by the few remaining bookmakers that will accept my bets). If therefore you feel an early price to be generous, you can take it having the security of knowing if the SP is bigger, you will be paid SP.

Betfred for instance also offer this service, but it doesn't apply to Lucky 15's, and some other multiple bets (or my bets, as they have withdrawn this feature on all of my bets, as well as restricting my stakes). They compensate the punter by offering three times the SP for one winner in a Lucky 15, against most other bookmakers who offer twice the SP.

One of my favourite bookmakers, was Paddy Power who will still accept my bets at the time of writing but to such small stakes, I no longer waste my time with them. They have something called a Justice Pay-out. Very simply if they believe that an event happening during a race has in some way affected the result through no fault of the horse or jockey; they will treat the bet as a void bet. I benefited from this on one occasion.

In one of my speciality races at Plumpton over 3ml 2f, there was a pretty poor set of runners. One of these was a horse called Bobbits Way, which was on offer the previous evening at 16-1 with Paddy Power. Now having studied videos of all the runners recent races, one piece of form stood out, a race at Bangor over 3ml 6f against a vastly higher calibre of jumpers. If you watch the race you will see he runs and jumps well until around half a mile from home when he is pulled up.

What's more his handicap mark had dropped by no less than 13lbs, since that run. He was also an Irish Point to Point winner in the past, and in one of his recent races he had been heavily backed. I was therefore more than happy to accept the 16-1 offered.

He started the race at odds of 7-1, and whilst the race was being run, I laid him at 6-1 and secured a matched bet. The third fence from home was dolled off because of a fallen jockey, and here Bobbit's Way joined the leader as they ran around the fence, the leader then leaned into him, forcing him off the course the wrong side of a running rail. At the time the air in room I was watching the race turned blue, although I had lost nothing as my bet was matched, I felt I had been robbed of what would have been a 10-1 winner (after allowing for paying my matched bet).

Later that evening I was more than pleased to find Paddy Power had applied there Justice Pay-out to my bet, making it a void bet.

The outcome being as I had lain off the original bet, when I had my stake returned, I was in profit on the day.

I hope this demonstrates clearly to you that you need to be aware of all bookmaker's specials and offers as they can increase your profits, providing they have the guts to accept your bets.

I have been insulted too many times by the derisory amounts they will offer to accept from me on my selections, that I no longer waste my time on approaching them for a bet.

WHAT IS VALUE?

Often in the racing press, much is discussed about a value bet. My definition of a value bet, is very simply, as a professional you should be able after studying a race to produce your own tissue for a race (i.e. what you anticipate the likely odds to be). If then the price of the horse which is your selection for the race, is more than two points longer than the price you anticipated, then you have your value bet. The next piece of advice I am going to provide you with takes a strong will, and a total belief in yourself as a successful gambler.

Very simply, if I have made my selection for a race, and my assessment of their form is that they should be on offer at 8-1. If the opening show with the early bird bookies is 10-1, then I will place a bet (if accepted), as I believe I have found a value bet. If the following morning, the same horse is on offer at 12-1, with either the bookmakers or the betting exchanges, then I will back him again. I will continue in this manner, every time the odds increase by 2 points or more, until I have reached my maximum stake* (I have a fixed sum that I will not exceed on **any** bet). I will also carry this strategy through to betting during the race, dependant on how I feel the horse is running.

The risk is of course that the stable are aware that the horse in question is not 100%, and this information has leaked, hence the lengthening odds. On the plus side the fact that you have invested heavily means you can offer longer odds than would have otherwise been possible, to ensure the bet is matched.

My experience of these occasions is that I am able to match up to 75%, of these bets, and on average one in six is a winning bet. Overall this has turned out for me to be a very profitable betting strategy. My greatest success with this strategy was in the Scottish National of 2008, I had backed Iris De Balme at 80-1, prior to the race. During the race he was on offer at 100-1, 120-1 and 140-1, all bets of which I was more than happy to accept. Unfortunately the layers offering these odds were only offering them for very small stakes, the smallest being a £5 bet at 140-1. Having secured many bets on the horse, I then immediately offered the horse at 40-1, all of my bets being matched with around 6 fences to jump. As you can see my strategy first and foremost is to avoid losing. I am never unhappy by giving away part of my possible winnings to protect my stake. This strategy has served me well over the years, because once your bet is matched, you can watch the race (or the remainder of the race if the bet is matched in running); totally relaxed by knowing you cannot lose whatever the outcome.

A common fault with many punters I have seen over the years is if they are backing an outsider, they will reduce their normal stakes because of the long odds. My advice is **"Don't do it".** If the majority of your bets are at level stakes then continue with this rationale with regard to outsiders. The size of your bet should represent the confidence you have in your selection, and the perceived value and nothing else. Please always remember that the horse has no idea of his/hers odds. If you find a 33-1 winner and you have been backing at level stakes, if you then back thirty consecutive losers you are still in profit. If I had a £1 for every time I have stood in a betting office and a punter has found a long priced winner, and then comments to all and sundry " I wish I had more on him, I was sure he would win", I would have more than doubled my betting bank.

You also need to be aware of poor value. Many horses represent poor value just because in the past they were ridden by Tony McCoy, or now trained by Paul Nicholls. This can however on occasions provide you with a bonus in terms of value, as if your selection is running in a race where the leading jockey of the day is riding, or Nicholls has a runner, it is more than likely that your selection is on offer at longer odds than it should be. This seldom affects me, as horses ridden or trained by them, only tend to appear in the long distance races I specialise in and only rarely in the races contested by the lesser rated horses.

*This does not apply to four in a row, which is in a later section.

FOUR IN A ROW

How many winning Yankees where you have you found four winners, in one day is a regular occurrence in your betting experience? Let me guess I bet they are few and far between. These days the only type of combination bet I tend to have is the occasional each way double, as I have found again after an analysis of my bets, that winning Yankees were as rare as hen's teeth.

The only major success I can recall in finding four winners on the same day, was for a lucky 15 to which I added a separate each way four timer being confident all would reach a place. Checking the results that evening on returning from a pig of a day at work, I was amazed to find all four horses were winners netting me sufficient for a holiday of a lifetime in Canada, together with a city break in Rome, and surplus spending money for both.

So around three years ago I developed a new set of rules to attempt to find regular accumulators of 4 winners in a row. Many of us will have a strong feelings after a serious bout of studying that we have found what to us is as near a certainty as is possible. This might happen anything between ten and twenty times a year for me, but seldom more, so I developed a new plan.

Again it is necessary to fund a bank, and for me I started modestly at £500, as I wanted to see how I progressed before committing more funds. You can start with any sum you feel is right for you.

The rules are as follows:

- Object is to find four winners, and if this is successful a new game is commenced to again find four winners. All bets throughout each sequence should be attempted to be matched.
- Opening bet is 5% of bank
- Once a sequence begins after the first winner, the original stake is doubled and placed on the second selection on horse 2, any further surplus being left in the bank.
- Should horse 2 also win, then again the stake is doubled and placed on horse 3, again any further surplus being left in the bank.

- Should horse 3 also win, then again the stake is doubled and placed on horse 4, any further surplus again being left in the bank.
- Win or lose after the 4th bet the sequence is commenced again with 5% of the bank being the opening bet, and a doubling of the maximum stake in each of the following winning bets. Each sequence then has a greater maximum bet than was allocated in game one, and by virtue of always retaining part of your winnings and any surpluses in your bank, the bank will have increased significantly.
- On the occasion where an each way bet is considered as a preference to a win bet, if the horse gets placed, this does not count as a winner and the betting sequence is commenced at the same stage, with the same stake.
- Any losing bet which was fully matched is ignored and the sequence recommences at the same stage, with the same stake.

This may sound complicated so to explain further, if your starting bank was £500, then 5% would be £25, and therefore the amount of your first bet. Following the sequence through your 2nd bet would be £50, your 3rd £100 and your 4th £200.

What this accomplishes by always increasing the level of the bank after each win, or a placed return, is that with only a modicum of success, the bank will grow, and when starting a new game, the initial stake of 5% of the bank will be much larger, at the commencement of each new game, and each subsequent bet would double.

After following this plan for just over three years, I have achieved three winning games with four winners in a row, but even where I have not had four winners in a row, the winners I have had have continued to increase the size of the bank, which is now very substantial, by virtue I believe, of my novel staking plan.

My most successful game was my last one, which was as follows:

Date	Selection	Odds Taken	Odds laid	Effective odds
09/12/2014	Sitting Back	16-1	6-1	10-1
27/12/2014	Royal McNab	7-1	3.5-1	3.5-1
16/02/2015	Paddy The Oscar	33-1	9-1	24-1
18/03/2015	Emma Soda	5.8-1	2-1	3.8-1

You can see that whatever your starting bank was and assuming you had made the same selections a very substanial profit would be achieved

Please remember that if you are successful with your selections, once your bets are over £100, you will experience problems placing them with bookmakers, so this is where the betting exchanges may probably be the only places you can place your bets.

As many of my bookmakers accounts are closed are restricted, if I wish a bet of £100 or more, and am unable to place the bet at the odds I require I have no other option but to go from betting shop to betting shop placing stakes of £10, while also utilising my Betfair account, until I achieve my optimum bet. The point you always have to keep at the forefront of your betting brain is that in many bookmaker's internet and mobile bets and some betting shops today, if you take a price and the starting price is returned at longer odds, your bet is settled at starting price.

Again be aware that betting shops are also monitoring closely any regular winning punters, and it is not unknown for shops to bar regular winners. At all times your prime aim should be to stay under their radar.

The reason I utilise bookmakers, instead of placing all my bets on Betfair where the only restriction is that there is enough in your account to cover your bets, is that many early prices offered by bookmakers are seldom not available on Betfair, except on some occasions to very small stakes. All of my subsequent lays are always placed on Betfair or Betdaq.

HOW I STUDY FORM

It may be useful for the reader to know how I study the form of my speciality area, and what is involved in a typical day.

1. At around 11-00am each day the declarations are available for the following day's racing. I first look through the cards to see if there are any races that conform to my speciality area.
2. If there are none, my day's work is complete
3. Conversely if any are within my speciality area I start work immediately

My routine is more or less the same each day but these are the actions I take. Not necessarily in the same order.

- Check my database to see if any horses are listed (usually I am already aware of horses declared, as I will have received an e-mail from the Racing Post that I have the horse listed in my Horse Tracker), and if they are I make a note of my comments.
- Check the *Chasers & Hurdlers Annual* and note any worthwhile information.
- Go to the *At The Races* website and check the *Timeform* notes on each horse, I then document any comments I feel to be relevant.
- Go to the *Racing Post* website, and check the *Stable Tour's Database*, this is where the trainers of some horses will have written what they feel about their horse, again note any relevant comments.
- Following on at the *Racing Post* website, I go through the horse form in detail, noting going, distance and course preferences, plus any aids (blinkers etc.). I will also look at their handicap rating, and whether it is on an upward or downward trend.
- Look at the comments under the spotlight notes, as soon as they are available, in the *Racing Post*, (unfortunately this is rarely available the night prior to the race, on their website until very late in the evening) again documenting any of the comments I feel to be relevant

- Check the trainers and jockey's current form, and their course record.
- View videos of past races to see for myself exactly how a particular horse performed.
- If the horse has Hunter Chase or point to point form, check his rating and the comments in the *Weatherbys* annual.
- Use *Viewpoint*, to watch any videos of ex point to pointers.

At this stage I will know whether I intend to get involved in any races, and if so I will have calculated what the minimum odds are I will accept, on any horse I intend to back.

Sometime after 5.00pm the early bird bookies will be advertising the prices on selected races. If any match the speciality races I intend to gamble on, and I believe the odds on offer to be value, I may place a bet at the odds offered (if I can get it accepted). I might add that time and time again I find the early bird bookies know little about the horses in my specialization area, and often offer ridiculous odds. A few seasons ago I availed myself of two 20-1 shots, which when the race commenced, both started as favourites. One went on to win and one lost, but on both occasions I was able to lay off my bet easily just before the off. The downside is that you only have to do this a couple of times, and the outcome is invariably the same, with the bookmaker closing the account.

Obviously I will also examine the situation with the exchanges, but at this early stage the odds on offer are rarely tempting, but I might place a bet offer at the minimum odds I would accept, and hope someone matches it as I sleep.

Once I have placed a bet I will decide what price I will offer to get my bet "matched", and I will ensure it is marked to keep the offer open during the actual race. Most of my matches occur during the race, with only around 12%, being matched before the race begins.

WHAT TYPE OF GAMBLER YOU NEED TO BE

Much is written about gambling in general, and we are all aware of compulsive gambling. I saw a quote recently which was:

"A compulsive gambler doesn't care whether he wins or loses, as long as he can gamble"

Similarly I saw this quote which I believe to be very true.

"Good Gamblers are bad losers"

This is why I believe the Golden Rule:

"Bet not to win but to avoid losing", is perhaps the most important rule if you want to make a success of your gambling. Taking less potential profit to protect your stake will in time provide greater levels of profit. Moreover it will not have the adverse effect on your confidence that a long losing run will almost certainly have.

I trust what I have written will help you become a more successful and disciplined gambler.

Good Luck.

25982100R00038

Printed in Great Britain
by Amazon